CAESAROMAGUS

A HISTORY AND DESCRIPTION OF ROMAN CHELMSFORD

by

Nick Wickenden

Keeper of Archaeology,
Chelmsford Museums Service

A CHELMSFORD MUSEUMS
SERVICE PUBLICATION 1991

CHELMSFORD
BOROUGH
COUNCIL

Published by: Chelmsford Museums Service, Civic Centre, Chelmsford CM1 1JE
ISBN No: 0 9518563 0 8

Front cover: Reconstruction of the Roman mansio at Chelmsford, by Frank Gardiner.

Printed by: THE PRINTING PLACE Ltd..., Empire House, Victoria Road, Chelmsford CM1 1PE
Facsimile: (0245) 267393   Telephone: (0245) 251001

CAESAROMAGUS

A Roman road map from the 3rd century AD, called the Antonine Itinerary, has survived the ravages of time and provides details of roads, towns and distances between them for many parts of the Roman Empire, including *Britannia*. There is a place *Caesaromagus* listed on two routes giving its distance from London as respectively 28 and 31 Roman miles, and the distance from *Caesaromagus* to *Camulodunum* (the early Roman provincial capital at Colchester) as respectively 24 and 21 Roman miles.

Scholars puzzled over the location of *Caesaromagus* for centuries, suggestions including Burstead near Billericay, Great Dunmow and Writtle. William Stukeley in

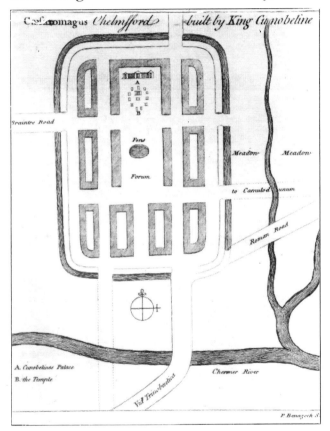

Fig.1 William Stukeley's imaginary plan of Roman Chelmsford, 1758

1758 correctly identified it as Chelmsford, but then drew a totally fictitious plan of the Roman town on the wrong (*north*) side of the river Can (Fig 1).

The truth became clear in the nineteenth century when Roman pottery, coins, burials and other finds were increasingly reported in Old Moulsham. Excavations in 1849 by Frederick Chancellor, a young architect later destined to become the Borough's first mayor in 1888 (Fig 2), revealed the first signs of the bath-house of the *mansio* - a large and impressive, state-run motel

Fig.2 Frederic Chancellor (1825-1918) - surveyor, amateur archaeologist, and the town's first mayor.

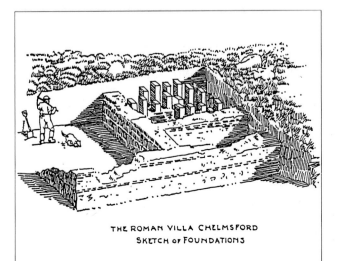

THE ROMAN VILLA CHELMSFORD
SKETCH OF FOUNDATIONS

Fig.3 Chancellor's sketch of his excavations in Moulsham in 1849, then in countryside.

occupying the whole of the south-eastern quarter of the town. This was the site of *Caesaromagus*, on the south side of the river Can (Figs 3 & 4).

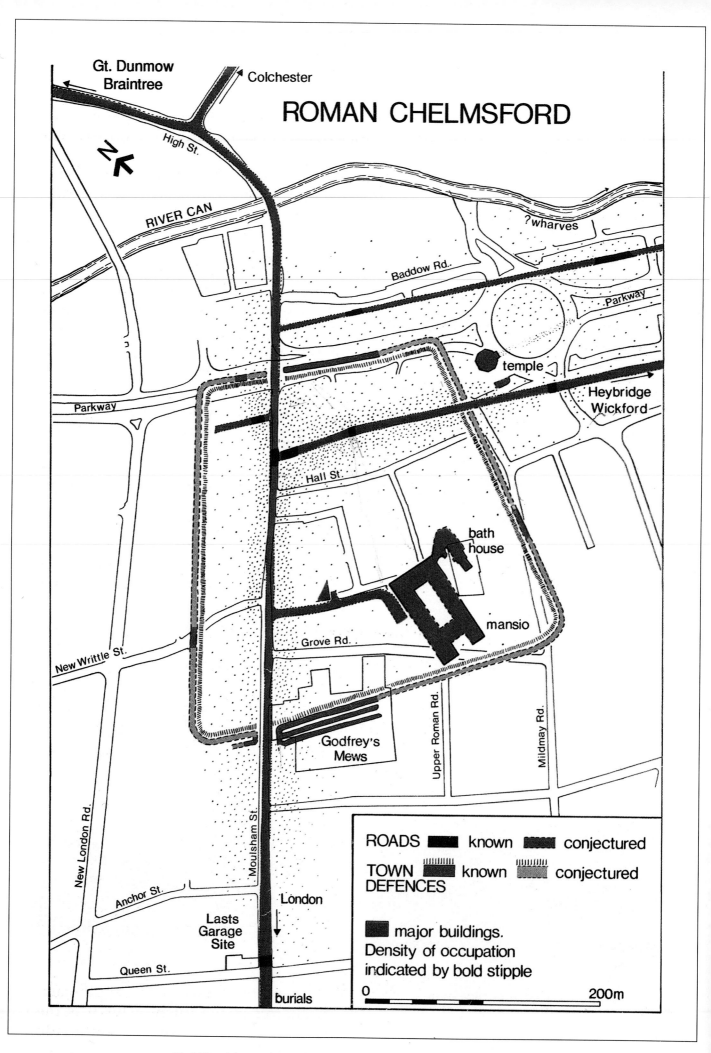

*Fig.4 Plan of the Roman town of **Caesaromagus,** overlaid on the modern town plan.*

Further excavations did not take place until 1947-49 when Major Jack Brinson unearthed more of the baths (Fig 5). It was the threat of the construction of the Inner Relief Road - Parkway - which prompted the formation of the Chelmsford Excavation Committee in 1968, and this group excavated some 40 sites in Chelmsford until 1978 when responsibility for new excavation passed to the newly created Archaeology Section of the Essex County Council Planning Department.

Fig.5 Major Jack Brinson (1911-1973), Roman Essex supremo from 1946 until his death.

The Excavation Committee (which later changed its name to Chelmsford Archaeological Trust) spent the years from 1978 to 1987 writing up and publishing the results of these excavations. Whilst not all the reports have yet been completed, the time is right to bring people up to date with what we now think Roman Chelmsford was like and how it developed. Recent work by the Essex County Council Archaeology Section has added to the picture.

Further work in the town may always bring new findings to light and make us change our thoughts.

Getting Your Bearings

It is worth stressing the small scale of the Roman town of **Caesaromagus.** Whilst Roman finds of pottery, tile, coins and other debris are often made in virtually any part of modern Chelmsford, the heart of the Roman settlement lay to the south of the River Can, roughly in the area enclosed by Parkway to the north, Mildmay Road to the east, Grove Road/Hamlet Road to the south, and the George Street car park to the west. In other words, a walk of 5 minutes along Moulsham Street would take you in and out of the Roman town!

The London to Colchester route of the old A12 largely follows the Roman road which ran along what is now Moulsham Street, across the river where the Stone Bridge is today, and along Springfield Road. Following Roman custom, the cemeteries of the town lined the main roads outside the built up area. They have not been systematically excavated in Chelmsford, but cremations have been found on the site of Dovedales College and in Rothesay Avenue off Moulsham Street.

A main side road ran eastwards out of the town, just to the north of Hall Street and led to a port at Heybridge. Roads to the north went to Great Dunmow and Braintree which both lay along Stane Street, the original Roman A120!

Pre-Roman Chelmsford

Fig.6 The pre-Roman, Iron Age village of round houses at Little Waltham in 1971.

The area enclosed by the rivers Lea, Cam and Stour - roughly what we call Essex today - was the tribal land of the Trinovantes with their capital at *Camulodunum* (Colchester). Their king until shortly before the Roman Conquest was Cunobelinus (Shakespeare's Cymbeline), who ruled virtually the whole of the south-east of England and minted coins at Colchester.

Iron Age man used to live in round-houses with walls of timber and daub with large conical timber roofs covered with thatch. A village of such houses was excavated in 1970-71 at Little Waltham, 6km (4 miles) north of Chelmsford, when the present day village was by-passed (Figs 6-7). This was in use from the 3rd to the 1st centuries BC, and much Iron Age pottery was found in the excavations, some of which is on display in the Chelmsford and Essex museum.

Until recently it was thought that the Roman town of Chelmsford was a brand new foundation, built on what was previously fields. However, excavations in the early 1970s east of Moulsham Street between Parkway and Hall Street revealed the plan of one complete round house and traces of the curving walls of others. It is now thought that there might have been a small settlement, perhaps no more than a farmstead, there at the time of, or shortly after, the Roman Conquest.

Fig.7 A reconstructed Iron Age thatched round house at Butser Farm, Hampshire.

The Roman Invasion

Fig.8 Coin of Claudius I, Emperor of Rome, AD 41-54.

The Romans had long had their eye on conquering Britain ever since Julius Caesar led two expeditions in 55-54 BC. However it was not until AD 43 that the emperor Claudius (Fig 8) sent 4 legions (some 40,000 men). The army landed at Richborough in Kent, crossed the Medway after a two-day battle, and marched into Essex and captured the British capital at Camulodunum, where they proceeded to establish their legionary base. Once installed, the legions split up to continue the conquest further west and north. Undoubtedly there would have been a network of smaller forts and temporary marching camps throughout Essex. Finds of military equipment (including part of a bronze horse harness pendant used by foreign auxiliary soldiers, Fig 9) and coins issued by Claudius to the soldiers are found in Chelmsford, but they are very difficult to date precisely . Even a 20 year span could include several major historical events. The weight of evidence indicates that the military foundation of Chelmsford was not part of Claudius' initial campaign.

The army, however, became complacent thinking that the local tribes had given up all resistance, and they even demolished the defences of their fort at Colchester to make way for a new town. The tribe of the Iceni, further north in Suffolk and Norfolk, rebelled under their warrior queen, Boudica, in AD 60-61 and swept through the south-east, destroying the new Roman towns of Colchester, London and St Albans before meeting defeat somewhere in the south midlands.

The Roman army did not make the same mistake again. A new network of forts was established at key points such as road junctions and river crossings to keep an eye on the local natives. It was at this point that they properly metalled the road from London to Colchester, passing through Chelmsford and built a fort south of the river crossing in Moulsham.

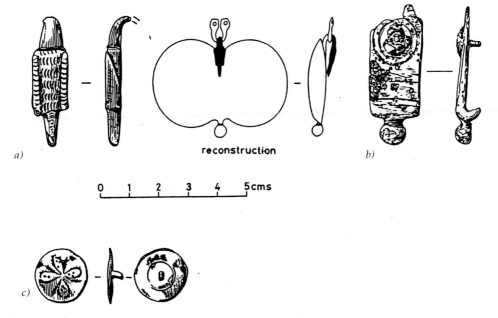

reconstruction

0 1 2 3 4 5cms

Fig.9 Military bronzes, lost in the AD60s.

a) the hook from a horse harness pendant.   b) a strap end   c) a stud end

The Fort at Chelmsford

Fig.10 Burial of a male pig on the site of the Roman fort in Moulsham - a sacrifice for good fortune?

Traces of wooden, post-built structures have survived from the earliest Roman levels; parallels in other parts of the country would suggest they belonged to military barrack blocks. Nearby a young male pig had been buried, possibly a sacrifice for the good fortune of the fort (Fig 10). Parts of a gravelled interior side street also survive - this was later to be incorporated into the town plan as the side street leading eastwards out of the town. This fort was built over the earlier round-house settlement, but was soon dismantled.

A second military enclosure, possibly a fort annexe or compound, has also been found on the site of Godfreys Mews in Moulsham Street. It was defended by

a bank and steep, V-shaped ditch, and enclosed 1.5 acres. Unfortunately no military buildings have yet been identified within this (Fig 11).

Outside both of these installations was a detached circular masonry feature - identified as a *Laconicum*. This was like a very hot sauna bath, and was also distinctly military in character (Fig 12). Its walls were of mortared bonding tiles, 60-90 cms wide,

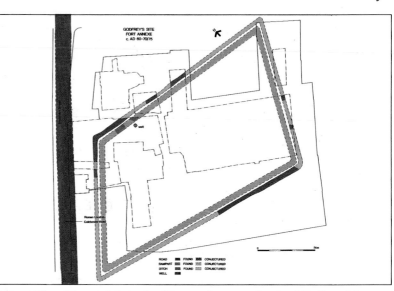

Fig.11 Plan of the quadrilateral military enclosure on the site of Godfreys Mews, Moulsham Street.

Fig.12 The circular **laconicum** or sauna, re-excavated in 1975.

and 7m in diameter. Like all baths, its floor (of a waterproof tile-chip concrete) was raised on little stacks of tiles so that hot air from an attached furnace could circulate underneath. Indeed the heat was often so intense that wooden clogs would have had to be worn to avoid burning the feet!

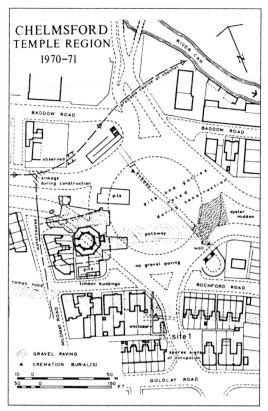

Fig.13 Excavating the temple region in advance of the Baddow Road roundabout in 1970-71.

Throughout its history, the main religious precinct for the town lay to the north-east, between Parkway, the Baddow Road round-about and Goldlay Road (Fig 13). This was probably initially used by the soldiers, and items of bronze jewellery, dedicated to the pagan Gods, have been found associated with the ditches of a ? sacred enclosure east of Mildmay Road (Fig 14). These offerings were probably hung on a wooden 'totem' pole or thrown down a 'wishing' well - both features were found in the excavations. A small length of masonry wall found at Goldlay Road may have been part of a late 1st century AD temple with an apsidal end (Fig 15).

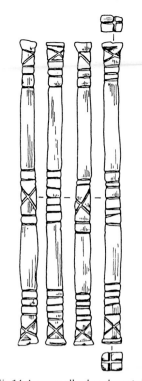

Fig.14 A copper alloy bar, decorated with lines and crosses, probably specially made as an offering to the gods.

Fig.15 Part of the later 1st century temple, and two possible reconstructions.

The Civilian Town

The forts at Chelmsford were only needed for ten years or so, and civilian houses and shops slowly established themselves in the new settlement, although there is evidence that the military were never far away from Chelmsford throughout its history. The name of the town - *Caesaromagus,* meaning the 'plain' or 'market-place of Caesar'- is still baffling, since it was a great honour for a town to have the imperial prefix incorporated in its name, and no other town in Britain was so honoured, yet Roman Chelmsford appears to have been only a middle-sized market town. It is possible that it was designed as a brand new tribal capital for the Trinovantes after the destruction of Colchester by Boudica; for whatever reason, however, Colchester resumed its pre-eminence and Chelmsford never assumed its mantle.

The Mansio

The fort-annexe on the site of Godfreys Mews became a military compound until about AD 120 when the area further east was developed as a *mansio*, or official guest house. These large buildings, comprising suites of rooms around a central courtyard, were built at regular intervals throughout the Province, on all the major roads; they were part of a programme, initiated by the emperor Hadrian, of remodelling the

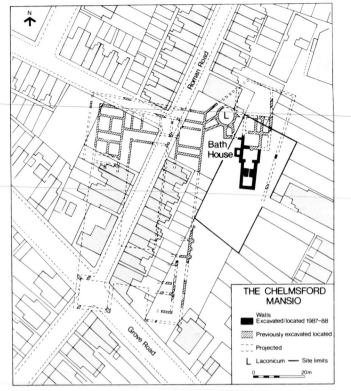

Fig.16 Plan of the mansio overlaid on the modern street plan. Note how many Victorian terraced houses would fit in its courtyard alone.

Cursus Publicus - that is the Department of Transport and the Royal Mail all rolled into one. The *mansio* was first built of timber, and replaced in masonry five years later. Its scale can be demonstrated by overlaying its plan on the modern street plan - a terrace of ten houses in Roman Road would fit in its courtyard alone!(Fig 16). Nothing of it survives above ground today, but the platform on which it was built,

Fig.17 The artificial terrace built by the Romans for the mansio; it still dictates the rise in the modern tarmac road.

created by terracing the ground, can still be seen as a slight incline in Roman Road (Figs 17-18). The mansio lay within its own precinct; a side road serving the building ran off the main road (Moulsham Street) (Fig 19).

Fig.18 Masonry footings of the mansio exposed in 1973.

Fig.19 Reconstruction of the mansio and its bath-house, lying within its own precinct within the town, by Frank Gardiner.

Fig.20 The mansio bath-house under excavation in 1987.

The *mansio* would have been furnished in the Roman way, to make the officials feel at home, and painted wallplaster and some pieces of mosaic flooring have been found (Fig 21). However, the furnishings were still pretty basic compared to the riches of the Continent or even Colchester. There were no fabulous marble floors here!

*Fig.21 Some of the mansio furnishings - painted wallplaster, tile and chalk mosaic **tesserae**.*

The complex had its own small temple and bath-block which was attached to the earlier military *laconicum*, and it was these baths that had been partially excavated by Frederick Chancellor and Major Brinson; indeed they were uncovered again in the 1970s, and the plan was only fully revealed in 1987 (Figs 20,22). The bath block contained a furnace, *caldarium* (hot room), *tepidarium* (warm room), and cold plunge.

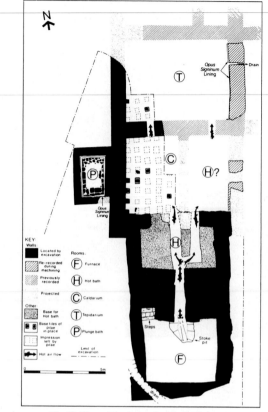

Fig.22 Plan of the hot end of the bath-house.

Underground wooden water pipes, probably leading from high water towers, supplied the mansio with running water. Although the wood has rotted away entirely, the iron bands connecting lengths of pipe have been found in excavations, still upright in their trench in their original positions! (Fig 23).

Both the *mansio* and its baths flourished for several centuries, and various amendments were made to the baths, which finally became derelict at the end of the 4th century when the furnace was choked with soot and ash. A timber outhouse was probably used for storing the wood needed for fuel.

*Fig.23 Iron water pipe collar lying **in situ** in its Roman trench. It would have joined two wooden water pipes, themselves long since rotted.*

Fig.24 Designs which would have been carved on a wooden roller, and used to impress box flue tiles before firing. The patterns were decorative, but also helped as a 'key' for mortar.

Some of the box flue tiles used in the hypocaust heating system were decorated with patterns carved on a wooden roller. These same patterns on tiles have been found elsewhere in the south-east of England, nearly always on important official Roman buildings and grandiose villas, and they seem to be trademarks of tilemakers used in official building contracts (Fig 24). A number can be seen in the Chelmsford and Essex Museum.

The Roads

The main London to Colchester road, built by the military in the early 60s AD, cut a straight path across Essex, and across the fort established in Moulsham (Fig 25). The side road was extended in the 2nd century, following the alignment of the early fort, itself probably based on Iron Age field systems, and both the mansio and the later temple followed that alignment rather than the line of the main road. This is still apparent in the modern town plan, explaining why roads like Baddow Road, Hall Street, and Anchor Street are not at proper right angles to Moulsham Street.

The roads were about 5m wide, built of layers of hoggin (coarse orange gravel) and sand, capped by a gravelled surface with a slight camber (Fig 26). This surface tended to

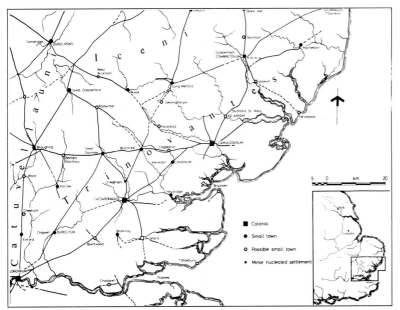

Fig. 25 The Roman 'County' of Essex was held by the tribal people called the Trinovantes. Map showing the major Roman roads, towns and villages.

get easily worn down and needed frequent maintenance. It provided a ready-made supply of gravel in the medieval period too! Either side of the road, wherever practical, was a drainage ditch. These also required regular cleaning, and we can see how buildings slowly encroached on the roadside verges requiring new ditches serving ever narrower roads to be dug.

Fig.26 Section through the gravelled side road leading eastwards off Moulsham Street; excavaed in the garden of the Prince of Orange public house in 1961.

13

Timber Buildings

The majority of buildings in Roman Chelmsford were built of timber with daub infilling. Where buildings burnt down, the clay with the impressions of wattles has been preserved, occasionally patterned with a roller. Roofs were mainly of thatch, although broken roof tiles are always found on digs suggesting some at least had tile roofs. The wooden beams of buildings itself have long since rotted away, leaving only stains or impressions in the ground if we are lucky. At worst, the buildings were constructed sitting on the ground level, so that no evidence except the areas of gravel or brickearth floors remain for the archaeologists to uncover.

However, where wood has lain submerged below the water table, it can survive, and some fragments were found in a Roman well in 1975. They formed part of a window frame, and the wall below the window, weatherboarded externally - so they probably would have looked quite familiar to our eyes. Windows were often glazed - fragments of the glass panes are sometimes found, and several have been reconstructed. These were protected by iron grilles.

Houses tended to be long and narrow, gable-end on to the road, jostling for space, especially in the 2nd century, when Chelmsford was probably at its busiest and most prosperous. The land behind the immediate street frontage contained rubbish and cess pits, wells, gardens and smaller sheds. At first land was divided up into plots, each plot defined by a boundary ditch on either side. A complete plot has been defined on the site of Godfreys Mews (Fig 27). Later on, plot boundaries were ignored as land was used to its maximum potential. A gravelled alleyway near the corner of Parkway and Moulsham Street, between two house plots, was itself built on with another house in the 3rd century. However, by the 4th century, more people were tending to move to the countryside as urban life started to decay; in Chelmsford some long 'halls' have been excavated, more reminiscent of Dark Age England, or the Netherlands, where the family and their farm animals all lived together under one roof.

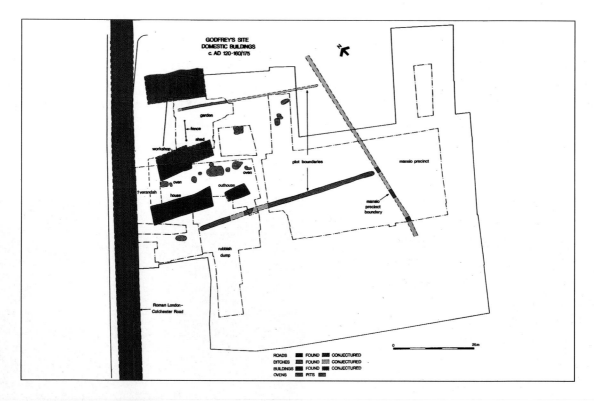

Fig..27 A complete house plot on the Godfreys Site, Moulsham Street, defined by shallow ditches (possibly a hedge); the plot contained a house, artisan's workshop, out-house, rubbish pits, ovens and a garden.

The Town Defences

In common with many other towns in the Province, Chelmsford was undefended and unenclosed for much of its life. But, for a short period from about AD160/175 to about 200/210, it was given defences of earthen banks and ditches. The reason was probably the threat of barbarian invasions from the sea and from beyond Hadrian's Wall. The defences were strengthened perhaps just before AD196 when a man called Clodius Albinus attempted to become Roman Emperor. His army consisted of many of the soldiers on permanent duty in this country, and there was a scare that in their absence the barbarians would take the opportunity to invade. Twenty years or so later the fears had temporarily passed, and some of the ditches on the Godfreys Mews Site were filled in and built over. Nevertheless there is evidence from several Essex settlements for widespread fires at the end of the 2nd century, possibly suggesting that for a while the barbarians did get the upper hand.

Fig.28 Military equipment lost in Chelmsford in the late 2nd century - two bronze horse harness pendants and a scabbard chape.

This operation must have taken a long time to carry out, and cost a lot of money and hard work It is probable that the defences were built by a detachment of soldiers either barracked in the town or brought in specially. Some of their lost or broken equipment has been found in excavations (Fig 28). The defences have only been partially identified and examined. In the south, on the Godfreys Mews site, three large parallel ditches have been found, each 2m (6 feet) deep (Figs 29-30). The outermost one may have continued to define the built up area of the town and was never backfilled. To the north the defences probably ran along the present line of Parkway, and they too do not appear to have been filled in again. Elsewhere in the town, the ditch has only been found in New Writtle Street and in builders works.

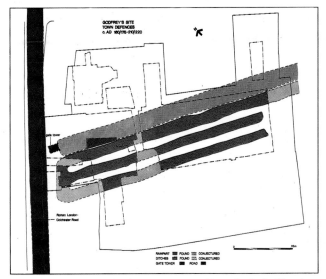

Fig.29 The triple ditched defensive system, and inner bank, flanking the southern entrance into the town.

Fig.30 The innermost defensive ditch, filled with the earth from the bank, thrown back in when the defences were no longer required.

Fig.31 A silver denarius of Septimius Severus, AD 196-7. Reverse Fortuna. Minted in Syria and found on the site of Godfreys, Moulsham Street, 1972

The Third Century

One problem faced by archaeologists in Essex is identifying 3rd century features. This may be because the pottery in use then has not yet been properly recognised, but it is generally believed that the 3rd century saw a contraction of the earlier building boom. At the end of the century, we do know that a building which had been built over the demolished defences on the Godfreys Mews site burnt down. This was a narrow timber-framed building of five rooms with a yellow clay floor. The charred remains of planks found were probably either part of the roof or an internal partition; the timbers were oak, and were infested with woodworm. Areas of burnt wattle and daub were found where walls had collapsed, and deposits of 'soot' were probably the remains of thatch - very few roof tiles were recovered.

Throughout the 3rd century, piratical raids from the North sea became more and more common. This was in part due to the deteriorating climate on the coast of Holland and North Germany, which forced the inhabitants there (the Angles, Saxons, Jutes and Frisians) to take to their boats in search of new homelands. The British fleet (or *Classis Britannica*) was crucial now in the defence of the Province. Indeed its admiral, a man called Carausius, for a while formed his own breakaway Roman Empire of Britain and Gaul, and minted his own coins; he was eventually murdered by his own finance minister.

To help beat off these piratical raids, a number of well-defended coastal forts were built in the later 3rd century from Portchester on the south coast to Brancaster in Norfolk. These forts were different in appearance to early forts and they looked much more like medieval castles. The defended coastline became known as the Saxon Shore; inland, Chelmsford does not seem to have been much affected, but Great Chesterford, near Saffron Walden, was in the heart of vital arable farmland, and was given massive new fortified walls.

The Fourth Century, the Temple and the Saxons

The mansio continued in use throughout the 4th century, probably functioning as the centre of administration, but generally the built up area of the town became less dense, and more land was given over to agricultural use, which caused a dark 'garden' soil to accumulate. However, life went on as usual, and around AD325 a very classy octagonal masonry temple was built in the religious precinct, where the Baddow Road roundabout is today (Fig 32). Only the foundations of this have survived because the masonry, so sought after in Essex because of a lack of natural building stone, had been removed at a later date for use elsewhere (Figs 33-34). Other temples of the same date and plan are known elsewhere in Britain and on the Continent - indeed, a similar one has only recently been found in London; the type is known as 'Romano-Celtic', and was used for the worship of pagan Gods, despite the introduction of Christianity as an official Roman religion by Constantine at about this time. Near the temple was found an animal rib bone carved with a person wearing a toga (Fig 35).

Fig.32 Reconstruction of the octagonal, masonry, Romano-Celtic temple at Chelmsford - the cut away shows the interior.

Pottery, glass and coinage indicate that occupation continued in the Roman town at least until around AD400, the date when the Roman army withdrew from Britain to consolidate what was left of their crumbling empire on the Continent.

Fig.33 The octagonal shape of the foundations - most of the masonry has been removed in antiquity.

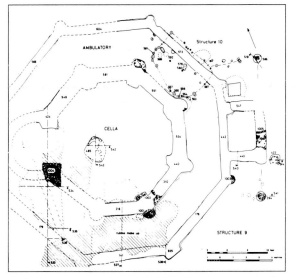

Fig.34 Plan of the octagonal temple, with opposing entrance porch and apse, where an image of the God would have been placed.

Undoubtedly people continued to inhabit the town for at least a generation, but it is a fact that virtually no Saxon pottery has been found within the Roman town. The Saxons nevertheless *were* in Essex; their houses have been discovered, amongst other places, in the heart of the Roman town at Heybridge, and in Colchester. But in general they shunned the slowly decaying Roman towns, and started their own settlements, perhaps because they were farmers rather than city dwellers. Their cemetery has been found at Springfield Lyons, and it is there that one should probably look for their settlement.

Fig.35 Bone plaque, made from a rib bone, carved with a toga-clad figure, possibly wearing a priestly head dress. From the Temple site.

The buildings of the Roman town would slowly have fallen into decay, and been used as a quarry for stone and tile, timber and gravel, slowly becoming more and more overgrown. The bridges or fords over the rivers Can, Chelmer and Wid, would have collapsed and become impassable, so that the main road eventually had to make a huge detour through Writtle. Moulsham did not see further building activity until the arrival of the Normans.

Death and Burial

Roman law forbade burying the dead inside the walls of towns, largely for reasons of hygiene; only infants were exempt from this; indeed excavations within the built up town have revealed baby skeletons buried in backyards. Because of this law, most Roman cemeteries are found straddling the roads outside the town gates (like the Appian Way in Rome), and Chelmsford was no different. The rite most favoured for much of the Roman occupation was cremation, and cremation burials have been found along Moulsham Street (Dovedales College and Rothesay Avenue), Broomfield Road (First Avenue) and on the Beachenlea Estate . The ashes were buried in pottery urns or wooden caskets, and often accompanied by platters and flagons which may have held food and drink for refreshment on the way to the afterlife. These pottery vessels were often deliberately broken in the belief that the dead could only use 'dead' pots. One particularly rich burial, dated to soon after the Roman Conquest, has been found at Little Waltham (Fig 36).

Fig.36 A cremation burial, comprising eight pottery plates, jars and flagons - the resting place at Little Waltham of a wealthy Roman or Romanised Briton around AD 50.

In the later 3rd and 4th centuries, people were also increasingly buried in coffins - the material used depended on the wealth of the dead person. Thus a poor person might be buried without a coffin at all; most people would have had wooden coffins, which have left no traces except where the iron nails holding them together have been found; stone and lead coffins were more expensive. Grave goods were sometimes included - that is, the dead would be buried with some of their favourite possessions - perhaps a brooch, hair pins, finger rings, even their boots!

In November 1987, contractors working on the site of Godfreys Mews uncovered a sandstone coffin and its occupant (Fig 37). This was unfortunately broken, but was carefully excavated and a second body was found by its side, not in a coffin but partially charred in a somewhat bizarre ritual (Fig 38). On this body were found a jet bangle and a tapering jet rod, possibly a priest's wand or symbol of office (Fig 39).

Fig.37 The discovery of a stone coffin (and occupant) during building work on Godfreys Mews in 1987

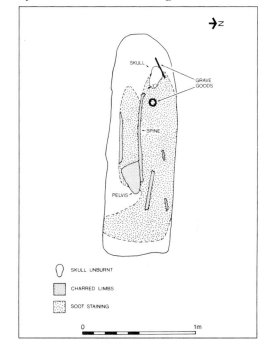

Fig.39 The jet bracelet and rod (possibly a priest's symbol of office) found on the burnt body

Fig.38 A second burial lay parallel to the coffin, the body had been burnt on a funeral pyre. A jet rod of office and a bracelet were found on the body.

There is some evidence that these two were buried on their own in a wooden mausoleum, and must have been VIPs in the town (Fig 40). The stone coffin has now been conserved and is on display in the Chelmsford and Essex Museum.

Fig.40 Reconstruction drawing of the funeral scene. The two burials probably lay within a large timber mausoleum.

The law was not always obeyed, though, and skeletons have been found inside the Roman town area, off Hall Street and Orchard Street. The famous hoard of Whitby jet jewellery on display in the Chelmsford and Essex Museum was found in 1972 off Hall Street and probably belonged to a wealthy 4th century Roman lady. The carving is of the highest quality and would have been made in York where Roman jet factories have been excavated (Figs 41-43).

Fig.41 The hoard of jet jewellery found buried in a wooden box in Hall Street in 1972.

Fig.42 The medusa head jet pendant.

Fig.43 The jet pendant depicting a lion holding a human head between its paws.

The Surrounding Countryside

Fig.44 Aerial photograph of the Roman villa discovered at Chignall St James in 1975.

As in the medieval period, Roman Chelmsford was primarily a market town where agricultural produce from the rich farmland in the vicinity would be sold or traded for other goods or services. Outside the town itself, which was quite small, there would have been isolated farms, larger private estates, and small villages. Such an estate was at Chignall St James where a large and imposing courtyard villa was discovered in 1976 by aerial photography (Fig 44). In this process, buildings and other features, such as ditches,

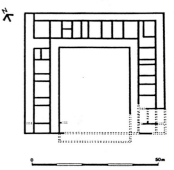

Fig.45 Plan of the villa at Chignall St James, drawn from air photographs.

can be seen from the air (though not at ground level), due to the crops, for instance, being distinctly parched where their roots have gone down onto the buried stubs of Roman walls (Fig 45).

Fig.46 Reconstruction drawing by Frank Gardiner showing the villa at Chignall St James within its working agricultural estate.

The villa itself has been scheduled by the Department of the Environment to preserve it; but excavations have taken place in the vicinity and located a barn, a small cemetery and a possible Roman vineyard! The building may have been the residence of an important local official (Fig 46). Another villa was probably at Plesheybury.

A small Roman village is known at Little Waltham, at the junction of Roman roads to Great Dunmow and Braintree. Discoveries include field ditches and house remains, a timber-framed well, a corn-grinding 'quern' or hand mill made out of puddingstone (a conglomerate stone from Hertfordshire), and a small cremation cemetery.

A new discovery, excavated in the summer of 1990, is a late Roman masonry building at Boreham (Fig 45). This had a massive tiled roof, and a large apse occupying the whole of its western wall. A general lack of finds seems to rule out its use as a villa or temple. It may have been the seat of a government official within an imperial estate, or, less likely, a Christian church.

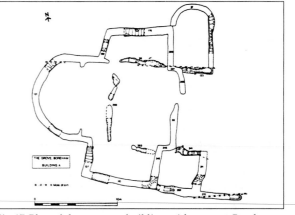

Fig.47 Plan of the masonry building with apses at Boreham.

Trade

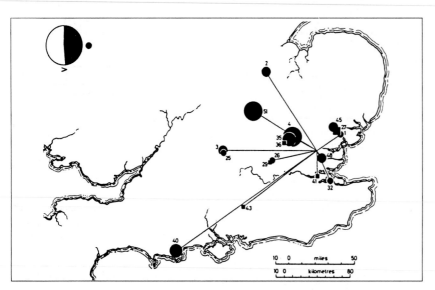

Fig.48 Pottery supply to Chelmsford, c AD 360/70-400+. Fabric numbers as follows: 1,27,45, Colchester; 2, Nene Valley; 3,25, Oxfordshire; 4,35,36, Much Hadham; 26,29, St. Albans; 32, North Kent; 40, Dorset; 41, Thameside; 43, Alice Holt; 48, Rettendon; 51, Bedfordshire.

Caesaromagus played its part in the trade networks of the Roman Empire, as shown by the finds made in excavations. Pottery was made in the town, but finer table wares were brought in from Colchester, St Albans, Much Hadham in Hertfordshire, Oxford, the Nene Valley near Peterborough, and North Kent. Extra special 'samian ware' with a fine orange-red glossy slip, and attractive moulded patterns, was shipped in from France and Germany; glossy black drinking beakers also came from Germany. Large pottery containers called 'amphorae' brought wine, olive oil and other delicacies from Italy and Spain.

Glass vessels, blown and coloured with great skill, came from North Italy, the Cologne area and probably even Alexandria. Lava from the Mayen area of Germany was turned into hard-wearing millstones and traded in great quantities.

From within this country came lead from the Mendips, iron from the Weald of Kent, shale from Dorset, jet from Whitby, and Millstone Grit from the Midlands.Essex does not have much naturally occurring building stone, save for flint and septaria nodules of hardened clay from around Dovercourt; tiles would have been made locally; some white ones were brought in from Kent. A vital commodity was salt, produced by the evaporation of salt water all along the coast of Essex on 'red hills', so called because of the vast amount of fired clay debris from the industry. Pieces of the clay evaporation tanks, called 'briquetage,' have been found in the town.

Coins found in Chelmsford also give a good idea of the trade networks at work, because each coin bears the abbreviation of the town where it was minted: places such as London, Arles and Lyons in France, Cologne and Trier in Germany, Rome and Aquileia in Italy, Siscia in Jugoslavia, and even Syria.

Religion

The Romans brought with them their own Gods and Goddesses, and built temples for their worship; they also worshipped certain emperors, who were deified after their death, as well as the spirit of Rome herself; at Colchester the temple of Claudius was the biggest in the Province, and was the most classical in appearance.

Elsewhere most temples are what is called 'Romano-Celtic' - a hybrid title since the Romans allowed each Province's native religions to continue as before, unless they were politically anti-Roman such as the Druids. Celtic religion was basically an out-of-doors affair, concerned with worship of natural phenomena like springs and forest groves; the Romans subtly matched up their own gods with the Celtic gods, so that eventually the native Britons were in effect worshipping Roman deities.

The most important temple in Chelmsford was probably the octagonal Romano-Celtic temple to the north-east of the town, though there may well have been others. Indeed we have seen how the 4th century temple was built on a religious precinct which had been in use since the 1st century AD. It may have been dedicated to the God Mercury, since there are connections with various animals known to have been associated with him; a small bronze figurine of a cockerel, for instance, was found in the *mansio*, and is on display at Chelmsford and Essex museum (Fig 49). Jaw bones found in rubbish

Fig.49 Bronze statuette of a cockerel found in the mansio. Possibly part of a larger group consisting of Mercury, surrounded by his favourite animals.

pits near the temple come from a specially bred herd of sheep (possibly for sacrifice).

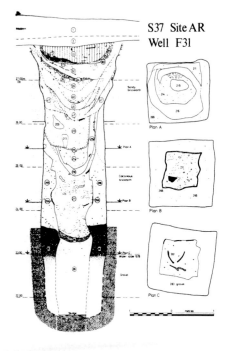

S37 Site AR
Well F31

In Orchard Street, a Roman well was discovered in 1977 which had been cleaned out on six different occasions. Each time, however, the new shaft bottom was *above* the water table, meaning that it was no longer being used as a well (Fig 50). In fact it was probably a ritual shaft used in Celtic religion and offerings would be poured down it. What the archaeologists found were dismembered horse and cow heads, new born lamb skeletons, raven and cat bones, and some human remains. Other horse heads in the

Fig.50 Celtic votive shaft, re-using a disused Roman well.

vicinity had been crushed. They may once have been displayed on poles. The cult seems to be connected with Epona - the Celtic Horse Goddess. A near complete horse skeleton was recently found on the site of Lasts Garage on Moulsham Street. It was unlikely that the horse had died from old age or disease, leaving ritual slaughter as a strong possibility (Fig 51).

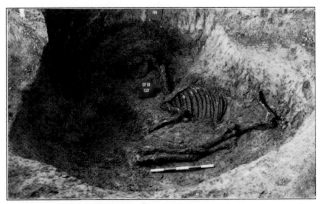

Fig.51 A complete horse skeleton - possibly a sacrifice - found on the site of Lasts Garage in Moulsham Street.

Fig.52 A pipe clay figurine of the Goddess Venus; large quantities of these souvenirs were imported into Britain in the 2nd century from central France.

The Romans also set up portable altars in their houses, and parts of several pipeclay figurines of the Goddess Venus have been found in the town; these were manufactured in central France in the 2nd century AD - several different moulds are known; it appears to have been quite a flourishing trade (Fig 52). Two other different pipeclay statuettes are also on display in the Chelmsford and Essex Museum (Fig 53).

Another find with religious significance is a folded up sheet of bronze embossed with a picture and gilded; only a spoked wheel can now be made out - possibly a votive plaque to Taranis - the Celtic God whose symbol was a wheel. Graffiti of wheels scratched on pots may have the same significance.

Fig.53 Two other pipe clay figurines from France, from the Chancellor Collection.

Fig.54 A greyware pottery bowl decorated with an applied snake, jaws agape.

One other find on the Temple site was a pottery bowl decorated with an applied, wiggling, open-jawed snake (Fig 54). Snakes were considered semi-divine, since they appeared to live in the ground and therefore were messengers from the underworld.

Christianity was made a legal Roman religion in the 4th century; up to then, Christians had been forced to practise in secret. Symbols such as the Chi-Rho (the first two characters in Greek of Christ's name), and the alpha and omega, have been found scratched on pots and tiles in Essex. A small church attached to a cemetery has recently gone on public view at Butt Road, Colchester. Chelmsford, too, may well have had a church in the 4th century, but it has so far eluded the archaeologists!

Literacy

Fig.55 Graffiti in Roman Chelmsford. Illiterates scratched simple 'X's but readable names include DISETE, IULITIO and BRITTA.

The official language of Roman Britain was Latin, though the average Briton would not have been very fluent, and probably continued to speak Celtic. Our best evidence for Chelmsford comes from scratched graffiti on pottery fragments -examples include an ABC being practised; DISETE, meaning belonging to Diseta; and most commonly an X, meaning I can't write but this is mine! (Fig 55). Correspondence was either on expensive papyrus, or on thin wooden wafers, or on wooden tablets with a recess, filled with wax: a fragment of this last type survives from Chelmsford, found in a well in 1975. The words were scratched in the wax with an iron or bronze **stylus**; if an error was made, the flattened end of the stylus could erase it (Fig 56). Part of a samian inkwell was found in 1969 on the site of Parkway. It even had an internal non-drip flange. Only one complete oil lamp has so far been found in Chelmsford (Fig 57).

Fig.56 All the necessary accoutrements for writing - a wooden writing tablet (reconstructed, with original fragment, left) iron styli, part of a Samian inkwell, and an oil lamp.

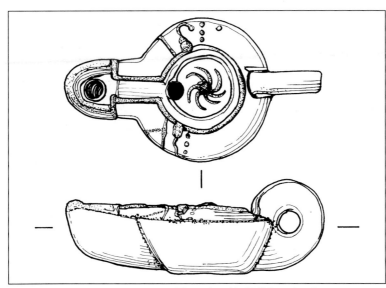

Fig.57 Greyware pottery oil lamp, found in Hall Street in 1975.

Industry

We must glean what we can about the trades that were practised in Roman Chelmsford from the rubbish thrown away by the traders themselves. Thus one fragment of leather found is an offcut from the back of a sandal, and we can therefore assume that both a tanner and a cobbler were at work. Iron smithing slag is a quite common find, so that we can assume that the smithy would have been a common sight, making and repairing all kinds of ironwork - nails, hinges, tools and fittings. Fragments of bronzeworking suggest that other metal smiths worked in the town, producing perhaps objects like brooches, hairpins, locks and keys, tweezers, nail cleaners and ear scoops - all of which have been found. A selection is on display at the Chelmsford and Essex Museum.

Fig.58 The timber frame, complete with corner rungs for added strength, of a Roman well, preserved due to constant waterlogging on the corner of Parkway and Moulsham Street in 1975.

Woodworkers made all sorts of bowls, combs, pulley wheels, ladders,etc, most of which rot away and are never found. Carpenters were quite skilled, however, and several timber-lined wells have survived, having been waterlogged ever since Roman times (Fig 58). The dovetailed mortice and tenons, and other joints, are really quite sophisticated.

Potters were also at work - not on the same scale as major industries in places like Colchester, but providing the everyday needs of the townsfolk, like cooking and storage jars, and bowls and dishes.Products of a kiln operating in the 1st century AD have been found near Goldlay Road. The kilns themselves of a 4th century potter were found on the Godfreys Mews Site in 1972 (Fig 59) - these were used to fire fairly plain greyware pots, tempered with sand and crushed flint after a fashion found in products of pottery kilns excavated at Rettendon and Sandon, and dated to about 260 AD and later.

Fig.59 Artist's reconstruction of a Roman potter at work in the 4th century. By Ronald Embleton.

Bone working would also have been practised, turning out hairpins, combs, knife handles and decorative inlaid shapes for boxes and so forth. The inlaid plaque from the temple site was carved with a Roman figure in a toga (Fig 35). The head of a bone hair pin was found at Chignall St James; it was carved with a ladies head, and clearly shows the fashion of her hairstyle (Fig 60).

It appears that one whole quadrant of the town, east of Moulsham Street from Parkway to Hall Street, was a complete bone processing plant in the 2nd and 3rd centuries AD. Cattle would be brought in from the countryside and slaughtered, dismembered and butchered; indeed, on the former site of Cramphorns in Moulsham Street, their hoof prints were found preserved in the muddy verges at the side of the road! (Fig 61). Every part of the animal was used: the skins were tanned for leather, and the horns were removed for horn-working. This was a skilled, but messy and smelly business; prolonged soaking in tanks was necessary to separate the useful horn-sheath from the core. Literally hundreds of the discarded cores have been discovered in excavations in this area - the smell as the horns lay rotting for months must have been quite overpowering.

Fig.60 The carved head of a bone hair pin, showing a ladies' coiffeur. Late lst-mid 2nd century AD.

It is possible that this would have been a military operation, since the army had need of a constant supply of meat, leather for dress, tents etc, and horn for equipment. If this was the case, perhaps the army had a permanent station in Chelmsford throughout its history - hence the importance of the mansio, and the construction of earthen defences in times of unrest.

Fig.61 Cattle hoof prints preserved in the muddy verges alongside Moulsham Street.

The museum's role

All the finds from the many different excavating campaigns, including the first by Frederick Chancellor in 1849, are stored in the Museums Service's reserve archaeological collection at the Old Cemetery Lodge, 1 Writtle Road, Chelmsford, CM1 3BL. They are maintained and curated there by the Keeper of Archaeology in a purpose-built archaeological store designed by Borough Council architects and constructed during 1989. A selection of the more complete and fascinating finds are on permanent display at the Chelmsford and Essex Museum, including many discussed and illustrated here.

Acknowledgements

Much of the results described here and illustrations are the work of the former Chelmsford Archaeological Trust which closed in March 1988. The majority of their excavations were directed by Paul Drury. More recent work has been undertaken by the Essex County Council Archaeology Section. I am particularly grateful to Patrick Allen, Alison McGhee, and the County Archaeologist, David Buckley.The text of this booklet grew out of a temporary exhibition, entitled *Caesaromagus- Quo Vadis?*, held at the Chelmsford and Essex Museum from 14 October to 26 November 1989. That exhibition, and half the cost of the conservation of the stone coffin, was kindly funded by Brookglade Properties Ltd, the owners and Developers of the Godfreys Mews site, and I am particularly grateful to Mr Chris Collins.

Further reading

Allen P. 1988   'Excavations of the mansio bath house, Chelmsford 1987-88', *Essex Journal*, vol 23.2, 27-33

Drury PJ 1988   *The mansio and other sites in the south-eastern sector of Caesaromagus*, Council for British Archaeology Report 66

Wickenden NP 1991 *The Temple and other sites in the north-eastern sector of Caesaromagus*, Council for British Archaeology Report 75

Illustration Credits

Bodleian Library, Oxford	1
Chelmsford Museums Service	2,3,17,19,28,39,40,41,52,53,54,55,56
Essex County Council, Archaeology Section	4,11,16,20,21,22,27,29,37,38,44,45,46,47,51,60,61
Essex Society for Archaeology & History	5
Mr. E Clack	6
Chelmsford Archaeological Trust	7,9,10,12,13,14,15,18,23,24,25,26,30,31,32,33,34,35,36,48,49 50,57,58
British Museum	8
Ancient Monuments Laboratory, London	42,43
Mr. C J Going	59